INVASION!

The
Normans

KAREN BRYANT-MOLE

Wayland

Invasion!

The Normans
The Romans
The Saxons
The Vikings

Cover design: Simon Balley
Book design: Malcolm Walker
Editor: Deb Elliott

Text based on *Norman Invaders and Settlers* by Tony D. Triggs published by Wayland Publishers Ltd in 1992.

Picture acknowledgements
Lesley and Roy Adkins 11 (top); Aerofilms 12; Ancient Art and Architecture Collection cover (all), 19 (top), 21, 23; ET Archive 29; Michael Holford 4, 6, 18 (bottom), 20 (bottom); Kobal 13, 18 (top); Topham 9 (bottom), 10-11, 26 (top), 28; Wayland Picture Library 8, 9 (top), 14, 15 (top), 19 (bottom), 20 (top), 22 (bottom); Tim Woodcock 22 (top).
Artwork: Peter Bull 5, 7, 15 (bottom), 26-7; Peter Dennis 16-17, 24-5.

First published in 1995 by
Wayland Publishers Limited
61 Western Road, Hove,
East Sussex, BN3 1JD

British Library Cataloguing in Publication Data
  Bryant-Mole, Karen
  The Normans. – (Invasion Series)
  I. Title II. Series
  942.02

ISBN 0 7502 1470 8

Typeset by Kudos Editorial Services
Printed and bound Italy by Rotolito Lombarda S.p.A.

Cover pictures:
Top left and middle right: Norman coins.
Top right: A brooch showing a griffin and a harpy.
Lower left: A thirteenth-century picture showing God measuring the world.
Bottom right: A section of the Bayeux tapestry.

Pictures opposite:
Top: A decorated Norman letter.
Middle: Some rich Norman people.
Bottom: A Norman castle.

Contents

THE NORMANS 4

WILLIAM'S KINGDOM........................7

CASTLES 10

INSIDE A CASTLE..............................13

ATTACK! 16

ANIMALS 18

BUILDINGS 20

A NORMAN VILLAGE 24

THE NORMAN AGE............................28

GLOSSARY 30

BOOKS TO READ 30

PLACES TO VISIT 31

INDEX 32

The Normans

The Normans came from a part of France called Normandy. Their leader was a duke, named William. In 1066, Duke William and his army sailed across the Channel to fight the army of the English king, Harold.

The picture below shows part of the Bayeux Tapestry. The Bayeux Tapestry is a series of pictures, sewn in coloured threads. The pictures tell the story of the Normans coming to England. This section shows some English soldiers on a hill-top and some Norman soldiers attacking them.

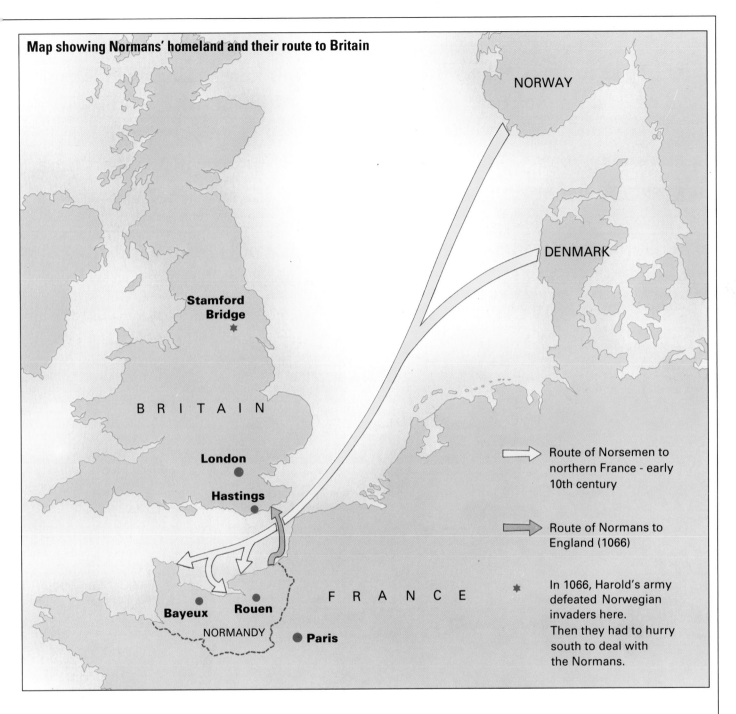

Map showing Normans' homeland and their route to Britain

Route of Norsemen to northern France - early 10th century

Route of Normans to England (1066)

In 1066, Harold's army defeated Norwegian invaders here. Then they had to hurry south to deal with the Normans.

The word 'Norman' comes from 'Northman'. The Normans were descended from people who had come to France from the northern countries of Norway and Denmark.

After landing at Hastings, on the south coast of England, the Norman army fought a battle against the English army. That battle is now known as the Battle of Hastings.

From 1042 to 1066, Edward the Confessor was king of England. When he died, Harold took over as king. But Duke William, who was Edward the Confessor's cousin, claimed that Harold had promised to help him become king when Edward died. William was furious when Harold broke his promise and became king himself.

The Normans defeated the English at the Battle of Hastings and King Harold was killed. Many people believe that he died after being shot through the eye by an arrow.

▲ There is a man with an arrow in his eye on the right of this picture from the Bayeux Tapestry.

William's kingdom

After winning the Battle of Hastings, William became king of England. He decided that, as king, he owned all the land and could share it out in any way he chose.

He let the churches use some of his land and kept some for his own private use. The rest of the land was shared out between his barons. These barons were usually rich followers and friends of William.

This map shows some of the land that the barons were allowed to use. Most barons had land in more than one part of the country.

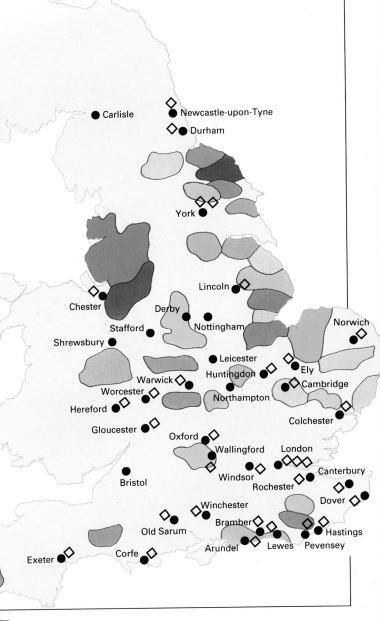

Areas of land held by different barons

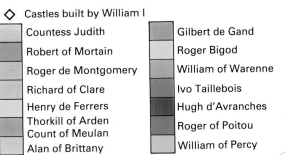

◇ Castles built by William I

Countess Judith		Gilbert de Gand
Robert of Mortain		Roger Bigod
Roger de Montgomery		William of Warenne
Richard of Clare		Ivo Taillebois
Henry de Ferrers		Hugh d'Avranches
Thorkill of Arden		Roger of Poitou
Count of Meulan		William of Percy
Alan of Brittany		

In 1086, William sent out messengers to find out as much about the country as they could. William wanted to find out how his land was being used. The messengers had to ask questions, such as how many pigs there were in each village, and how many people rented land from the barons.

All this information was written down in two books. Together, the books are known as *Domesday Book*.

▼ Two pages from *Domesday Book*.

Picture stories

The woman in the picture below is looking at the Bayeux Tapestry. The Bayeux Tapestry told a story in pictures. You could try this, too, by drawing a series of pictures on the back of an old roll of wallpaper.

Think of a title for your story and write it on the wallpaper. You could also decorate some of the letters.

▲ A decorated letter.

Castles

Many of the Norman barons built castles to protect themselves and their land. They often built these castles on the top of a hill.

▲ The Norman castle at Chepstow in Wales.

▼ The Norman castle at Ludlow in Shropshire.

▲ The wooden parts of this castle have disappeared. We know a castle once stood here because we can still see the ditches.

At first, Norman castles were very simple.

They were made by digging a circular ditch. The earth from the ditch was piled into the middle of the circle, making a mound, called a motte. A wooden tower, or keep, was built on the motte. A second ditch was built around the first ditch. You can see the two ditches in the picture, above. The ground in between these two ditches was called a bailey.

Later, bigger and stronger castles were built from stone.

Inside a castle

This picture shows how the inside of a Norman castle might have looked. This is the main room, or great hall. There would have been a wood fire in the middle of the hall.

▲ The big stone halls of Norman castles were used for meetings and eating meals.

The Norman landholders enjoyed hunting. The person in this picture has a hawk on his arm. Hawking was a popular way to hunt. Some large hawks could catch pheasants and even geese! Bows and arrows were used to hunt for wolves, boar and deer, too.

Food was usually cooked in kitchens but sometimes meat was roasted over the fire in the great hall. The baron and his family ate their meals from long wooden tables. They used their fingers to eat most of their food.

A picture from a Norman book. ▶
It shows a man on horseback
leaving a castle.

A Norman recipe

People might have eaten a dish like this in Norman times.

Ask an adult to help you cook it.

1 Boil some cubes of meat in water.

2 Roll out some pastry.

3 Mix the cooked meat with grated cheese and a beaten egg.

4 Shape it into balls.

5 Wrap the meat balls in pastry and bake in the oven.

6 Pour a spicy sauce over the cooked meat balls.

A Norman monk drinks some wine from a barrel.
▼

Attack!

The Norman barons were sometimes attacked by other barons who wanted more land.

The attackers would try to capture the baron's castle. They used huge wooden catapults to throw large rocks across the moat, hoping that these would damage the castle walls. Sometimes, a large tree trunk was used to break down the castle door.

But most Norman castles were very well built. As long as the people inside had food and water, they could stay there for months.

Animals

Horses were very useful in Norman times. They were used in battles, for hunting, for travelling around the countryside and even for sport.

This is a modern photograph of a Norman sport called jousting. Two men on horseback rode towards each other with long poles, called lances. Each man tried to knock the other off his horse.

▲ A group of men hunting, on the Bayeux Tapestry.

This picture shows a different kind of jousting, called quintain jousting. The man on the horse tried to hit the shield of the wooden man. The wooden man would spin round. The rider had to move away quickly or he would be knocked off his horse.

▲ Jousting was a way for Norman men to practise fighting.

Women looked after all the animals that a family owned. They milked the cows and sheep and collected eggs from the hens. Women also had to look after the garden, spin wool, make butter and cheese and take care of their children.

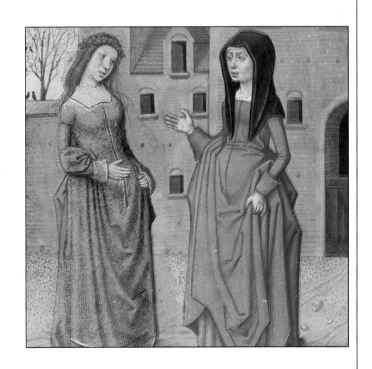

Some women in Norman times wore clothes like these. ▶

Buildings

Religion and churches were an important part of Norman life.

The picture below shows what is left of a Norman priory. Monks used to live in this building.

▲ An important priest speaking to people in the open air.

▲ The ruins of a priory at Castle Acre in Norfolk.

▲ This photograph shows a town house in Lincoln that belonged to a Norman merchant. It is one of the oldest houses in Britain.

Most English people lived in small villages. However, during Norman times, more and more towns began to develop.

Some towns were built by rich landholders. Some grew up around castles or churches. Many grew up around the markets that villagers travelled to.

► A manor house.

The areas of land that William let his barons use were called manors. The main house on each of these pieces of land was called the manor house. The person who lived in the manor house was known as the lord of the manor.

The lord of the manor let the villagers use some of his land. The farmland in each manor was divided into strips. The villagers were given a number of strips in each field.

▼ Men and women harvesting a strip of wheat.

The villagers had to pay the lord of the manor for the use of the land. They paid in money, goods or by working for the lord of the manor.

At harvest-time all the villagers had to give some of their crops to the lord of the manor and some to the church.

These crops were stored in a barn called a tithe barn. This is a photograph of a Norman tithe barn.

A Norman village

This is how a Norman village might have looked.

The manor house was made of stone. It had several outbuildings. In the courtyard there was a well. The white, bell-shaped objects next to the house are bee-hives.

The villagers' homes were made from wooden frames filled in with a muddy mixture, known as daub. The roofs were covered with long grasses, called rushes.

This village also had a stone church with a square tower.

Make a map

You could draw your own
Norman village. This map ▶
is from *Domesday Book*.

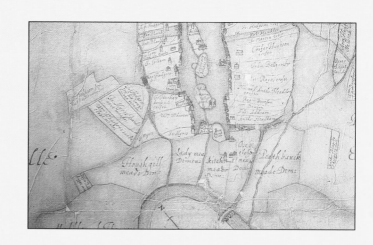

Start by drawing in the cart tracks.

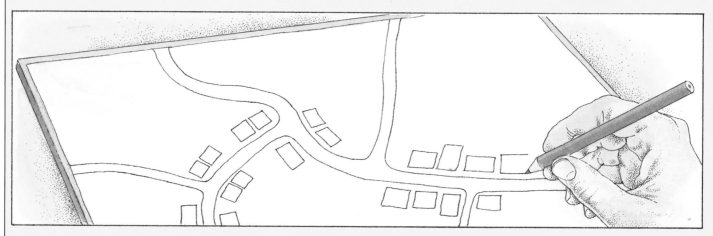

Draw boxes where you would like the houses to go.

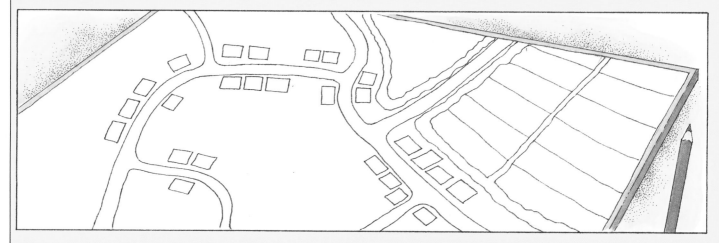

Now, draw in some fields, divided into strips.

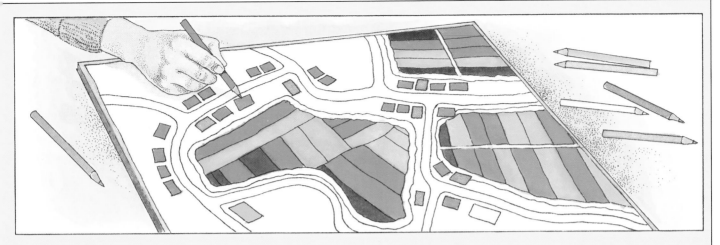

Use several different colours to colour in your map.

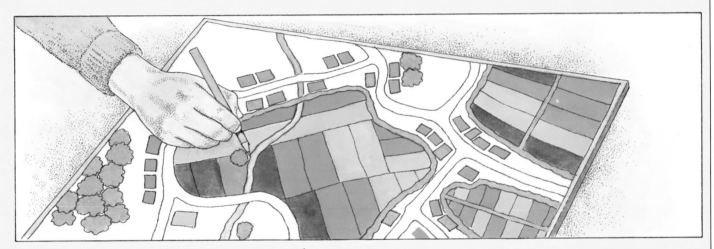

You could add in some trees and a stream.

Try to make your picture look as real as possible.

The Norman age

As this book has shown you, some Norman homes and buildings are still standing today. Some Norman objects can still be found, too.

The stone font in the picture below was carved during Norman times. This font is in a cathedral. Many Norman objects are now in museums. You may be able to see some Norman objects in a local museum.

Buildings, objects, books and drawings have all helped us to find out about the way people lived in Norman times.

A stone font in Winchester Cathedral. ▼

▲ The four Norman kings.

William was the first Norman King of England. When he died his son became king. He was also called William and was known as William II.

William II was killed by an arrow while hunting. His brother, Henry, then became Henry I.

When Henry died, William I's grandson, Stephen, became king. He was the last of the Norman kings.

The chart below tells you when they reigned.

1066	1087	1100		1135	1154
William I ('the Conqueror')	William II	Henry I		Stephen	Henry II

The Bayeux Tapestry made.

Domesday Book made.

War between Stephen and Henry I's daughter Matilda.

| The Norman Kings |

Glossary

barons   Rich people who were given land by the king.

cathedral   A very big church.

font   A big bowl for water in a church, used for baptising a baby.

harvest   Gathering in crops that have finished growing.

hunting   Chasing and killing animals, for food or for sport.

landholder   Someone who owns land.

moat   A ditch filled with water that surrounded a castle.

merchant   Someone who buys and sells things to make money.

monks   Men who followed a religious way of life.

priory   A religious building, rather like a monastery or abbey, where people live and worship God.

Books to read

Norman Britain by Tony D. Triggs (Wayland, 1990)

The Normans by Peter Chrisp (Wayland, 1994)

The Normans by P. Rooke (Macdonald, 1987)

Norman Castles by Graham Rickard (Wayland, 1989)

Yound Researcher - The Normans by H.M. Martell (Heinemann, 1992)

Places to visit

If you would like to find out more about the Normans, or see some remains of Norman life, you could visit the following:

Bamburgh in Northumberland: castle

Bungay in Suffolk: castle

Canterbury in Kent: cathedral and Eastbridge hospital

Castle Acre in Norfolk: castle, priory and town remains

Castle Rising in Norfolk: castle and church

Dalmeny in Lothian: church

Dunfermline in Fife: church

Durham: castle and cathedral

Ely in Cambridgeshire: cathedral

Fountains in North Yorkshire: remains of a monastery

Inverurie in Grampian: castle

Lincoln Cathedral

London: British Museum, Museum of London, Tower of London, Victoria and Albert Museum

Lumphanan in Grampian: site of castle

Much Wenlock in Shropshire: castle

Norwich in Norfolk: castle, cathedral and 'Music House' in King Street

Old Sarum in Wiltshire: site of castle and cathedral

Pembroke in Dyfed: castle

Rievaulx in North Yorkshire: abbey

St Davids in Dyfed: cathedral

Southampton: houses and town wall

Tyninghame in Lothian: church

Index

animals 18–19

bailey 12
barons 7–8, 14, 16, 30
Battle of Hastings 5–6, 7
Bayeux Tapestry 4, 6, 9, 18
buildings 20–7, 28

castles 10–13, 14, 16–17, 21
catapults 16
cathedrals 28, 30
churches 7, 20–1, 23, 24

Domesday Book 8, 26, 29

Edward the Confessor 6

farms 22–3
food 14–15

harvest 23, 30
hawking 14
horses 14, 18–19
houses 21, 24–7, 28
hunting 14, 18, 30

jousting 18–19

King Harold 4–6
King William I 4–8, 22, 29

land 7–8, 22–3

manors 22, 24
maps 26–7
moats 16, 30
monks 20, 30
motte 12

Norman kings 29

priory 20, 30

religion 20

soldiers 4–6

towns 21

villages 8, 21, 24–7

women 19